Race Films:
50 Years of Independent African American Cinema

Second Edition

By Jeremy Geltzer

Also by Jeremy Geltzer
Behind the Scenes: A Child's Guide to Film History
Charlie's Little Tramp: The Life of Charlie Chaplin
Oscar Micheaux: A Self-Made Man

Published by the Hollywood Press
hollywood-press.com
First Edition December 2014

Table of Contents

1

What Are Race Films?

Underworld (1937)

Even before Hollywood became a motion picture-producing powerhouse, a different type of movie had begun to develop. While studio-made films appealed to worldwide audiences, the actors were almost always white. Race films served as a counterpoint. Race film producers made pictures featuring African American actors in stories that appealed to African

American audiences and spoke directly to the black community. These films catered to an audience that mainstream motion picture ignored.

Race films emerged at a time when America was divided. Mainstream theaters delivered blockbusters to local screens but often restricted black audiences or sent them to upper rows of the balcony. As an alternative, theaters in black neighborhoods opened their doors to create what became known as the "chitlin' circuit."

Sepia Cinderella (1947)

Theaters along the East Coast, across the South and Mid-West were safe and acceptable for African American entertainers and audiences during the era of racial segregation. The most famous show house on the circuit was the Apollo in New York City. Along the East Coast, other stops included the Uptown Theatre in Philadelphia, the Howard Theatre in Washington D.C., and the Hippodrome Theatre in Richmond. In the South, Atlanta's Royal Peacock, Birmingham's Carver Theatre, and Jacksonville's Ritz Theatre were top venues. Heading into the Mid-West, key stages included the Regal Theatre in Chicago, the Fox Theatre in Detroit, and Madam C. J. Walker's Theatre in Indianapolis.

Before motion pictures arrived, these theaters teemed with musicians, comedians, and vaudeville acts. When movies became the rage, the "chitlin' circuit" playhouses were primed to feature a different type of film than what studio films had to offer. African American filmmakers rose to the task of creating an alternative to Hollywood. The charismatic and prolific Oscar Micheaux is the best remembered of these filmmakers but there were many others, including William Foster, the Johnson brothers and Spencer Williams.

THE LINCOLN MOTION PICTURE CO. (Inc
PRESENTS

"BY RIGHT OF BIRTH"
FEATURING
CLARENCE BROOKS
ANITA THOMPSON AND WEBB KING.
IN A NEGRO ROMANCE OF LAUGHTER AND TEARS.

Killer Diller (1948)

Race films grew out of a segregated system that divided audiences. From this divided beginning, African American filmmakers crafted their own screen icons that delivered swinging music, hilarious comedy, and provocative melodrama. Race films thrived during the silent era but the arrival of talkies in the late 1920s changed everything.

Sound technology required a higher degree of expertise and made movies more expensive to produce. Still, race films were able to survive for another two decades—even reaching a second Golden Age

with musical and dance films in the 1940s. Everything changed after Sidney Poitier made his feature film debut in *No Way Out* (1950). Poitier's talent and popularity proved African American performers could no longer be restricted to minor roles as maids and servants or relegated to a separate cinema of race films. Poitier's success represented a move toward racial integration but it was also a nail in the coffin of race films and the industry of the separate cinema.

If the industry of race films began with William Foster in 1913, it ended with Poitier in 1950. Once Poitier blazed the trail for African American performers as leading players in mainstream Hollywood, the separate cinema of race films was shattered. The era of race films ended.

While Poitier opened a door it would be another 50 years before African American actors such as Denzel Washington, Will Smith, Jamie Foxx and Idris Elba were able to support studio tentpole productions. Half a century after the era of race films was ended by integration, many of the talents, studios, and films have been lost and forgotten. The legacy of race films were overlooked by mainstream history for decades and allowed to disintegrate. This book will help to resurrect

forgotten film figures and restore the memory of the men and women—the dancers and comics and cowboys and leading actors and athletes and torch song singers who wrote their own names among the stars to become screen legends against all odds.

2

Beginnings

Bert Williams in rediscovered footage, c. 1914

Even before race films existed, African American performers had been seen on screen. In the pioneering days of motion pictures, most roles for black actors were demeaning stereotypes. Racist comedy shorts showed boxing bouts, dancing step shows, and eating contests. Then, in 1898 an Edison cameraman named William "Daddy" Paley presented a glimpse of African Americans in a different light.

William "Daddy" Paley (1843-1924) was a British cameraman-inventor. In the 1890s, Paley developed a device called the Kalatechnoscope and opened picture parlors to compete with Edison's Kinetoscope. By the middle of the decade Paley closed his operation to join Edison Manufacturing Company as a roving cameraman. In 1898 Edison sent Paley on assignment to cover the Spanish American War.

Colored Troops Disembarking, (1898),
Edison Manufacturing Company

Paley set off for Havana Harbor where he rolled film on several actuality-documentaries: *The Wreck of the Battleship Maine* (1898), *Burial of the Maine Victims* (1898), *Roosevelt's Rough Riders Embarking for Santiago* (1898), and *The Battle of San Juan Hill* (1898). Among his dispatches from the front lines, Paley included a subject entitled *Colored Troops Disembarking* (1898). The picture showed the 2nd Battalion of Colored Infantrymen marching down the gangplank from a steamer. For the first time on film African Americans were seen on film outside racist portrayals.

African American troops, c. 1898

The scene proved popular and was almost immediately duped by pioneering producer Siegmund Lubin. Lubin's Pennsylvania-based film factory released *Colored Invincibles* (1898). The studio's catalog described the reel as "the famous colored troop, the so-called immunes, who went away to fight with as much zeal as their white brothers."

The U.S. film industry began in earnest with the explosion of nickelodeons and the success of Edwin S. Porter's *The Great Train Robbery* (1903). Along with this famous heist picture, Porter also offered the first film adaptation of *Uncle Tom's Cabin* (1903). The title was profitable enough for Lubin to make his own version in 1905.

ELIZA PLEADS WITH UNCLE TOM TO RUN AWAY.

The Vitagraph Company produced their own all-star remake in 1910 featuring then-marquee names Florence Turner and Flora Finch, along with soon-to-be-silent-stars Maurice Costello, Ralph Ince, Norma Talmadge, Earle Williams, and Clara Kimball Young.

FLOGGING OF UNCLE TOM.

The Everlasting Play

THE W. Griffith Co.

Present

Uncle Tom's Cabin
(5 REELS)

Star Cast Includes
Julia Swayne Gordon
Ralph Ince
Carlyle Blackwell
Florence Turner
others

The Story that will Live Forever.

Distributed and Controlled by The W Griffith Co. 145 W 45 th St New York City

Uncle Tom's Cabin proved to be a fan favorite at the box office. New Rochelle, NY-based studio Thanhauser Film Corporation released a version of *Uncle Tom's Cabin* in 1910. Kalem's star director, the globe-trotting Sidney Olcott, offered his own reworking in 1913. I.M.P./Universal assigned Otis Turner, the director who had adapted *The Wizard of Oz* in 1910, to produce a version of *Uncle Tom's Cabin* in 1913.

While *Uncle Tom* was a crowd-pleasing title, one black performer was achieving pop culture celebrity: Bert Williams. Williams (1874-1922) had risen to become one of the preeminent Vaudeville entertainers of the era.

Williams had been performing with his partner George Walker since the mid-1890s. They headlined Koster and Bial's venue for 36 weeks during the same season Edison introduced his motion picture attraction.  Both the performers and the producers understood the synergy of the act and the technology. By 1901 Williams & Walker recorded a series of discs for the Victor Talking Machine Company.

A decade later, Biograph filmed but never released a movie entitled *Bert Williams Lime Kiln Club Field Day* (1913). This is the oldest existing film with an all-black cast and the footage provides a glimpse behind the scenes of early filmmaking. *Field Day* was rediscovered, restored, and revived at New York's Museum of Modern Art's 12th Annual To Save and Project Festival in 2014-2015.

Before the discovery of *Field Day*, only three Bert Williams films were known to exist: *Darktown Jubilee* (1914), *A Natural Born Gambler* (1916), and *Fish* (1916). Shellacked in blackface, as was the custom of the time, Williams was able to overcome demeaning race comedy: in a top hat, raggedy overcoat and oversized shoes. His character is reminiscent of Charlie Chaplin's tramp, who was also achieving great popularity at the time. Today Bert Williams is a forgotten film star, best remembered as a stage comedian, songwriter, and recording artist with his chart busting single "Nobody." But the recently discovered footage shows the promise of an early entertainer that rose above the race restrictions of his era.

The pioneering motion pictures of Bert Williams set the stage for African American performers to take control of their own screen images. A series of independent black filmmakers, many based in Chicago, would take the next step.

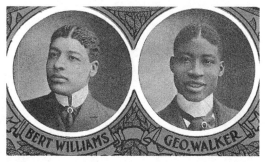

Sources

"Notes Written on the Screen" in *The New York Times,* August 23, 1914.

"Bert Williams Dies Here After Collapse on Detroit Stage" in *The New York Times*, March 5, 1922.

Felicia R. Lee, "Coming Soon, a Century Late: A Black Film Gem" in *The New York Times*, September 20, 2014.

Steven W. Thrasher, "Oldest Surviving Film With An All Black Cast Moved Me to Laughter and Tears," in *The Guardian*, October 27, 2014.

3

Early African American Studios: 1915-1920

Oscar Micheaux directing

Operating out of Chicago, William D. Foster (1884-1940) blazed new trails by establishing the first African American-owned and operated film studio: the Foster Photoplay Company. Foster produced his first short picture, a slapstick comedy entitled *The Pullman Porter*, in 1910. This marked the first time a black director supervised an all-black cast. *The Porter* was made by a black man for a black audience—race films were born.

Foster followed *The Pullman Porter* with a series of knockabout comedies: *The Railroad Porter* (1912), *The Fall Guy* (1913), *The Butler* (1913), and *The Grafter and the Maid* (1913). The next year he toured the chitlin' circuit with his program. The response was so enthusiastic that he planned to build a studio in Jacksonville. But after producing one more picture, *The Barber* (1916), Foster Photoplay collapsed. William Foster briefly reappeared in Hollywood a decade later directing a series of black musical shorts for Pathé, but his days as a pioneering filmmaker were behind him.

Across town in Chicago the Ebony Film Company opened its doors. Ebony was a white-owned studio that began producing race films featuring African American performers in 1915 just after Foster's films proved popular. The studio saw race films as a potentially lucrative sub-genre marketed to a particular demographic.

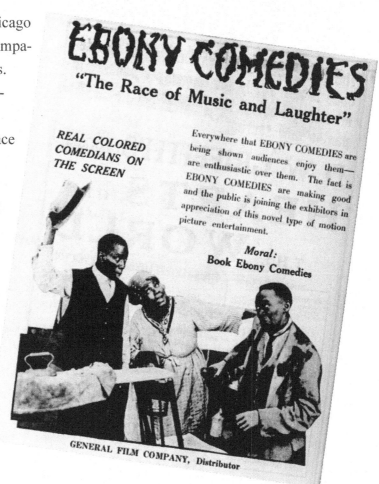

EBONY COMEDIES

"The Race of Music and Laughter"

REAL COLORED COMEDIANS ON THE SCREEN

Everywhere that EBONY COMEDIES are being shown audiences enjoy them—are enthusiastic over them. The fact is EBONY COMEDIES are making good and the public is joining the exhibitors in appreciation of this novel type of motion picture entertainment.

Moral:
Book Ebony Comedies

GENERAL FILM COMPANY, Distributor

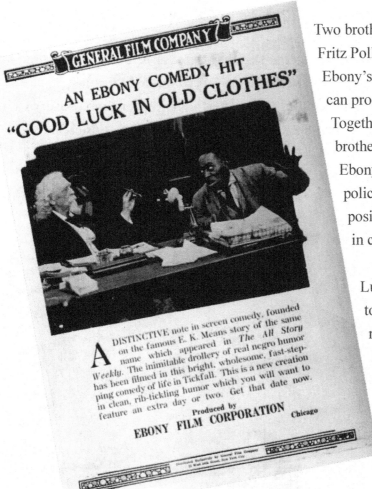

Two brothers, Luther and Fritz Pollard were hired as Ebony's African American product managers. Together the Pollard brothers re-calibrated Ebony's race film policy to advocate positive black images in cinema.

Luther (1878-1977) took over corporate responsibilities as well as directorial duties. Fritz (1894-1986) handled creative aspects and managed talent and casting. Between 1915-1918 Ebony produced over 20 two-reel comedies including *Two Knights of Vaudeville* (1915), *Aladdin Jones* (1915), *Money Talks in Darktown* (1916), *Shine Johnson and the Rabbit's Foot* (1917), *Devil for a Day* (1917), *Good Luck in Old Clothes* (1918), *The Comeback of Barnacle Bill* (1918), *A Black Sherlock Holmes* (1918), and *Black and Tan Mix Up* (1918).

By 1918, Ebony announced a series of integrated comedies that featured black and white players. This was one step too far. *The Chicago Defender*, a newspaper that catered to African American readers, attacked Ebony's move. *The Defender* was relentless and became one factor that led to the shuttering of the studio in 1922.

Set apart from the Chicago race film-scene, the Lincoln Motion Picture Company incorporated in Omaha. Founded in 1915 by two brothers, Noble (1881-1978) and George Johnson (1885-1977), Lincoln became the first major black-owned film studio. Lincoln planned their production slate just as a small town named Hollywood, CA was attracting studios. Following the trend, Lincoln quickly rented production facilities in Los Angeles. Unlike the white-owned Ebony, which was looking for box office bucks, the Johnson brothers's stated purpose was to "encourage black pride."

FEATURING NOBLE M. JOHNSON

Makes You More Money And Satisfies Your Patrons

Displaying Beautiful Photographs of Your Favorite Star Means Perpetual Popularity and More Profits For You

They Will Prove Effective on Your Walls in Your Lobby, on Your Programs and as Souvenirs

Place Your Order Now While Low in Price

Twenty-one Plays One Hundred and Thirty-one Reels at your Option

Every Single Reel Spells PROFITS

LUBIN
"Mr. Carlson of Arizona" 3 reels.

UNIVERSAL
Regulars
"The Heart of a Tigress" 3 reels.
"The Lion's Ward" — 3 reels.
"The Indian's Lament" 3 reels.
"Who Pulled the Trigger" 3 reels.
"Lady of the Sea" 1 reel.
"Last of the Night Riders" 2 reels.
"His Master's Wife" 3 reels.

Features
"The Soldier of the Legion" 3 reels.
"The Caravan" 3 reels.
"Emerald-Cumbler" 3 reels.

Red Feather Specials
"Fighting for Love" 5 reels.
"Love Affairs" 4 reels.
"The Terror" 5 reels.
"Mr. Dolan of New York" 5 reels.
"The Hero of the Hour" 5 reels.

Serials
"The Red Ace" 36 reels.
"The Bull's Eye" 36 reels.

LINCOLN
Lincoln Features
"The Realization of a Negro's Ambition" 2 reels.
"The Trooper of Troop K" 3 reels.
"The Law of Nature" 3 reels.

NOBLE M. JOHNSON
"The Favorite of Millions"

This is the opportunity you have long desired; so get busy. Write, wire, phone or call your local exchange. If no results, place your requests in writing with the

PUBLICITY MANAGER
OMAHA, NEBRASKA 2816 PRATT STREET OMAHA, NEBRASKA

Lincoln's first film was *The Realization of a Negro's Ambition* (1916). It starred Noble Johnson as a college educated man who leaves his girlfriend and his father's farm to seek his fortune out West. He is initially denied employment at an oil field because of his race. But after saving the boss's daughter he is accepted into the company. The man rises through the corporate ranks and returns home to realize that his father's farm sits atop an oil reserve. Instantly a wealthy self-made man, he marries his old sweetheart. The film's message of self-reliance, persistence, and following one's dreams to achieve goals appealed to black audiences.

Lincoln's next production was a more ambitious project: *A Trooper of Company K* (1917). *Trooper* followed the ripped-from-the-headlines story of an all-black cavalry unit's battle against the better-equipped Mexican Army in June 1916. Although the Fighting 10th sustained heavy losses, they inflicted even more damage on the Mexican troops. The Buffalo Soldiers even took out their opponent's commanding officer. Countering the offensive message seen in *The Birth of a Nation* (1915), *Trooper K* showed heroic black soldiers on the battlefield.

Above, the Lincoln Motion Picture Company, Noble Johnson (center), George Johnson (second from right); *The Law of Nature* (1917) was third film produced by the Johnson brothers.

In the wake of *The Birth of a Nation* and the series of war films that followed, *A Trooper of Company K* had the makings of a black blockbuster. Adding to the picture's authenticity, Lincoln was able to hire a large cast that may have even included ex-troopers who fought in the actual battle.

Trooper caught the eye of Universal Pictures executives who sought out the film's leading man. The studio signed Noble Johnson to be their on-staff exotic player. Over the next 33 years Noble would play hundreds of native roles at Universal, including Friday in *Robinson Crusoe* (1922), Queequeg in *Moby Dick* (1930), and the Native Chief in *King Kong* (1933).

With Noble's departure, the Lincoln Film Company continued under the guidance of George Johnson. They produced *The Law of Nature* (1918) and *A Man's Duty* (1919). Next George prepared another "important" picture called *By Right of Birth* (1921), which featured Booker T. Washington in a cameo role. At the Los Angeles premiere over 1000 people purchased tickets that were priced between $.50-$1.00. Reviews were positive: one paper wrote: "The Lincoln management

Noble Johnson as the native chieftain in *King Kong* (1933), top, and as Ivan in *The Most Dangerous Game* (1932), both directed by Ernest B. Schoedsack for RKO Pictures.

is due considerable credit for their ability to handle a six-reel photoplay typically racial in appeal, yet free from radical propaganda such as has been characteristic in several similar productions." The film was educational and well-reviewed but it lacked commercial appeal. Prestige alone could not keep the small studio afloat. *By Right of Birth* would be Lincoln's final film.

While William Foster receives credit as the first African American motion picture producer and Lincoln as the first important black-owned studio, the late 1910s saw a boom for race filmmakers.

The Chicago Defender hailed Peter Jones as the leading African American still photographer of the day. Jones composed portraits of leaders such as Booker T. Washington and W.E.B. De Bois as well as

African American infantrymen in World War I

panoramic shots of black landmarks and neighborhoods. Between 1914 and 1916 Jones was able to fund a filmmaking unit and incorporated the Peter P. Jones Photoplay Company. At first he focused on newsreel-type subjects, such as *For the Honor of the 8th Illinois Regiment* (1915) and *Negro Soldiers Fighting for Uncle Sam* (1918).

Jones Photoplay next project, *The Slacker*, was a narrative film centered on a black anti-hero. *The Slacker* (1917) told the story of a draft dodger that comes to terms with his civic duty. As a filmmaker Peter Jones showed promise. Then in 1922, Hollywood producer Lewis J. Selznick hired Jones to run his New York-based film lab and the Peter P. Jones Photoplay Company was closed.

Chicago remained a hotbed of African American film talent. In 1918, The Birth of a Race Photoplay Company released their own cinematic response to D.W. Griffith's *The Birth of a Nation*. *Birth of a Race* was presumed lost until a print was rediscovered in the 1980s. Another producer, Virgil L. Williams established The Royal Gardens Motion Picture Company in 1919. Royal Gardens produced *In the Depth of Our Hearts* (1920). This film's theme focused on the tension between light-skinned African Americans and those with darker complexions and was praised by *The Chicago Defender*.

White-owned race film factories were also competing for screen time. The Democracy Photoplay Corporation put out *Injustice aka Democracy or a Fight for Right* (1918). Another white-owned studio called Delight Film Corporation was preparing a production in 1919 when Lincoln Pictures dispatched corporate spies for inside information. The Johnson brothers discovered that there was little to fear when Lincoln's informers reported that, "the whole place looks like a swindling joint."

As Hollywood's studios were setting down their foundations—Universal in 1912, Fox in 1915 and Famous Players-Lasky (Paramount Pictures) in 1916, African American filmmakers were already demonstrating their own vibrant film community. Chicago was the center. Starting with William Foster more than half a dozen black filmmakers churned out race films from the Windy City. While the late teens showed promise, the race film industry would grow even more lively during the next decade.

Segregated movie theater in Mississippi

Sources

Davarian L. Baldwin, <u>Chicago's New Negroes: Modernity, the Great Migration, and Black Urban Life</u> (Chapel Hill: University of North Carolina Press, 2007).

Torriano Berry, Venise T. Berry, <u>The 50 Most Influential Black Films: A Celebration of African-American Talent, Determination and Creativity</u> (New York: Citadel Press, 2001).

John M. Carroll, <u>Fritz Pollard: Pioneer in Racial Advancement</u> (Chicago: University of Illinois Press, 1998).

Michael Corcoran, Arnie Bernstein, <u>Hollywood on Lake Michigan: 100+ Years of Chicago and the Movies</u> (Chicago: Chicago Review Press, 2013).

Barbara Tepa Lupack, <u>Literary Adaptations in Black American Cinema: From Micheaux to Toni Morrison</u> (Rochester: University of Rochester Press, 2002).

Charlene Regester, "Early African American Pioneers in Independent Cinema: From Humor as Camouflage to Provocation as Revelation" in <u>African Americans and Popular Culture</u>, Todd Boyd, ed. (Westport: Greenwood Publishing Group, 2008).

4

The Golden Age of Race Films

Richard Norman behind the camera.
Courtesy of Norman Studios Silent Film Museum and Norman Family

The 1920s were the Golden Era of Hollywood silent film—major studios controlled the industry and jazz age art deco style was the craze. "Modern" women could dance, smoke and speak their minds. Mostly overlooked, the work of black filmmakers also saw a Golden Age during the 1920s. Around the country race film producers made movies aimed at empowering their audiences, offering positive images of successful and upwardly mobile black heroes.

Based in Jacksonville, the Norman Film Manufacturing Company released an impressive slate of eight pictures between 1920 and 1928. Since the earliest days of the film industry, Florida had been the winter hub for production. Major studios such as Edison, Kalem, Lubin and Selig as well as early independents such as King

Courtesy of Norman Studios Silent Film Museum and Norman Family

Bee, Metro, and Vim set up southern stages. By 1916 Jacksonville supported over 30 studios. Four years later when California established itself as the film capital, Jacksonville's reputation as a motion picture production destination stalled.

In a facility abandoned by Eagle Films, Richard E. Norman (1891-1960) moved in and opened Norman Films. Norman was a white man, an aspiring filmmaker having produced a few pictures such as *The Green Eyed Monster* (1916). Incorporating Norman Films in 1919, he shifted focus to race films and particularly the presentation of upright and respectable black heroes and heroines. Norman's first picture was a spectacular all-black version of *The Green Eyed Monster* (1919).

The following year Norman took his film crew to the all-black town of Boley, Oklahoma. In Boley, Norman signed Bill Pickett (1870-1932), a Texas cowboy and rodeo performer. Since 1905 Pickett had been a top attraction at county fairs. Traveling with the Miller Brothers' 101 Wild West Show—a troupe that included Buffalo Bill, Tom Mix, and Will Rogers—Pickett's act showcased his skill at bull-dogging. In his bull-dogging stunt show, Pickett would grab cattle by the horns and wrestle the livestock to the ground. Norman hired Pickett to appear in two motion pictures: the aptly titled *The Bull-Dogger* (1921) and a follow up, *The Crimson Skull* (1922). These were the earliest all-black westerns.

Courtesy of Norman Studios Silent Film Museum and Norman Family

A decade later the daredevil cowboy died after suffering a kick to the head during his act.

Pickett was gone but Norman Films continued to bring exciting African American adventure flicks the screen. In *Regeneration* (1923), Norman filmed a shipwreck story with a pirate's treasure twist. One year before Paramount produced *Wings* (1927), Norman

Courtesy of Norman Studios Silent Film Museum and Norman Family

released *The Flying Ace* (1926) inspired by Bessie Coleman, the first licensed black female pilot. Norman discussed making a picture with Coleman but their dream ended when she died in a plane crash in April 1926. The film was rewritten to feature Laurence Criner as a WWI pilot returning home to resume his former job as a detective. Norman promoted the picture as "the greatest airplane thriller ever filmed" but the thrifty producer actually used shots of a single plane from different angles slickly edited to create aerial dogfights. The scenes still thrilled.

32

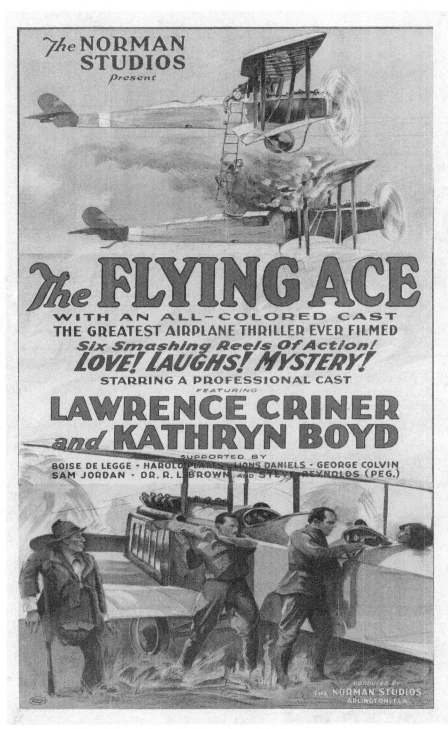

Courtesy of Norman Studios Silent Film Museum and Norman Family

Courtesy of Norman Studios Silent Film Museum and Norman Family

Courtesy of Norman Studios Silent Film Museum and Norman Family

Criner also starred in Norman's next picture, a western oil drilling saga called *Black Gold* (1928). This would be Norman's last production; talking films had arrived and his small studio could not afford the transition to new technology. Norman pivoted out of film production to instead distribute race films made by other producers along the Southern chitlin' circuit. After Richard Norman died in 1960, his studio and its legacy were forgotten. Four decades later, Ann Burt, a Jacksonville resident discovered that several local dilapidated buildings on Arlington Road had once housed a film studio. A preservation group was formed and in 2002 the facilities were restored and transformed into the Norman Studios Silent Film Museum.

Another important location was New York City, where film producers could draw from the great talents already contributing to the Harlem Renaissance. The Lafayette Players Stock Company, formed in 1916, was one of Harlem's first commercially successful black revues. The troupe's stage manager was Robert Levy (1888-1959), a white London-born Jew. Within five years Levy branched out to form a film division and market 'high class' pictures featuring Lafayette's well-known performers. Reol Productions was launched in 1921.

Reol provided a contrast to the leading African American filmmaker of the day: Oscar Micheaux. Micheaux produced popular potboilers. He was a relentless self-promoter that was always in need of financing for his films. Levy, on the other hand, was more interested in artistic, professional productions. And he was well connected to investors. From its base in New York, Reol opened

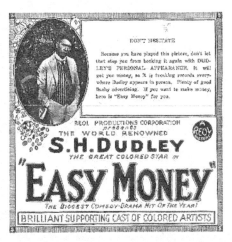

distribution offices in Chicago, Dallas, Atlanta, and Cleveland. Between 1921 and 1926 Reol produced 12 uplifting melodramas including *The Burden of Race* (1921), *The Call of His People* (1921), *Secret Sorrow* (1921), *The Sport of the Gods* (1921), and *Easy Money* (1922). Censorship records and lobby cards suggest that Reol's comedy *The Jazz Hounds* (1921) borrowed from Ebony Film's popular Black Sherlock Holmes character. Despite Reol's industry influence and importance at the time, the company has faded into obscurity to become a forgotten footnote in the history of race film production in the United States. No films produced by Reol are known to exist.

Reol Productions catalog: *The Secret Sorrow* (1921), *The Burden of Race* (1921), and *The Schemers* (1922). All films have been lost.

Grace Smith and Juano Hernandez in *The Girl from Chicago* (1932), above, Cab Calloway and Jeni Le Gon in *Hi-De-Ho* (1947), below

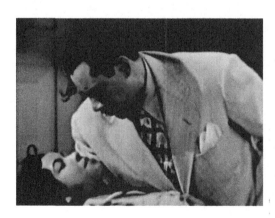

A LIST OF COLORED FILM PRODUCING COMPANIES

Lincoln Motion Pictures Co., 1121 Central ave., Los Angeles, Cal.

Micheaux Film Corp., 538 South Dearborn st., Chicago, Ill.

Reol Production Corp., Robt. Levy, pres., 126 West 46th st., N. Y. C.

Bockertee Film Co., 1718 West Jefferson st., Los Angeles, Cal.

Democracy Film Corp., 1718 West Jefferson st., Los Angeles, Cal.

North State Film Co., Ben Strasser, mgr., Winston-Salem, N. C.

Norman Film Co., 1614 Laura st., Jacksonville, Fla.

Aydlauer Productions Co., Ozark Bldg., Kansas City, Mo.

Gate City Feature Films, 1701 East Twelfth st., Kansas City, Mo.

Afro-American Film Exhibitors, 1120 Vine st., Kansas City, Mo.

Monumental Pictures Corp., 1816 Twelfth st., N. W., Washington, D. C.

Maurice Film Co., High and Antoine sts., Detroit, Mich.

West Motion Picture Co., Boston, Mass.

Delight Film Co., 2139 S. Wabash ave., Chicago, Ill.

Mount Olympus Dist. Co., 110 West 40th st., New York City.

The Del Sarte Film Co., Clarence Muse, director, 1919 Broadway, New York.

Royal Garden Film Co., 459 East 31st st., Chicago, Ill.

In 1921, a year before they closed shop, Reol approached a successful stage performer and veteran vaudevillian named Sherman H. "Uncle Dud" Dudley (1872?-1940). Levy arranged for Uncle Dud to bring his popular character to the screen in *The Simp* (1921). As Reol faded from the scene Uncle Dud found a new producer.

Uncle Dud teamed with David Starkman, the white owner of a black theater in Philadelphia, to form the Colored Players Film Corporation. Starkman-Dud's mission was to make films that catered to black middle class urban audiences. Colored Players first picture was *The Prince of His Race* (1926). This was followed by their masterwork, *The Scar of Shame* (1927). *Scar* explored levels of social status that existed within the black community. In the film Alvin, wealthy young concert pianist rescues the beautiful Louise from her squalid life. They marry but Louise is shattered when she learns Alvin has

hidden their marriage from his family, ashamed of her lower breeding. When a gangster shoots Louise, she is left with a hideous scar and ultimately commits suicide, paving the way for Alvin to remarry a better-suited upper class woman. *The New York Times* called *Scar* "quite possibly the best independent black film of the silent era."

Despite positive reviews and commercial success, Colored Players Film Corp. only made one more film, *Children of Fate* (1928) before closing their doors. Once again, the likely cause of the studio's demise was the cost of transitioning to sound pictures.

While the mainstream motion picture industry was centralized in two locations: production in California and corporate in New York, islands of race filmmakers made movies around the country. A Kansas City-based still photographer named George W. Curtiss (1865-1936) toyed with moving pictures and produced the city's first film, a documentary short "actuality," in 1897. Less than 20 years later the small city saw a mini-production boom. William Andlauer, a white theater manager and budding producer, hired Curtis as a newsreel producer.

Meanwhile, another Kansas City outfit, Progress Picture Producing Association released the first feature film made locally, *The Lure of a Woman* (1921). *Lure* featured A. Porter Davis, a pioneering African American aviator and upwardly mobile professional with a medical degree. Progress Pictures planned a series of eight films but all that survives are scenes from the studio's second project: *The Human Devil*. It is not known whether *The Human Devil* was completed or released.

Meanwhile Andlauer Film Company decided to compete with Progress. Moving into feature race film-making, Andlauer hired the former world heavyweight champion boxer, Jack Johnson (1878-1946), to appear in *As the World Rolls On* (1921). Reviews indicate that the picture fused a melodramatic plot with a daring robbery and even scenes of a National Colored League baseball game—the Kansas City Monarchs versus the Detroit Stars. The surviving footage of minority sports stars Sam Crawford, Rube Foster, and Bruce Petway add to the film's value as a valuable historical document.

A decade earlier, in the 1910s, Jack Johnson had appeared in several successful boxing pictures including the "Fight of the Century," which was recorded by Vitagraph and released as *Jeffries-Johnson World's Championship Boxing Contest, Held at Reno, Nevada, July 4, 1910* (1910). Johnson was controversial as the first African American

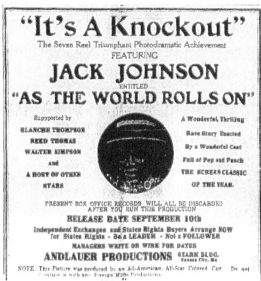

heavyweight boxing champion. His films were scandalous not only because boxing films were in the process of being banned by the states but also because mainstream audiences didn't like seeing their hometown heroes and white pugilists put down by the towering African American champ. Johnson was so popular that he headlined several more fight films: *Johnson vs. "Fireman" Jim Flynn* (1912), *Johnson vs. Frank "The Fighting Dentist" Moran* (1914) and *Johnson vs. Jess "the Pottawatomie Giant" Willard* (1915). In the 26th round of a bout fought in Havana Cuba, Willard took the title from Johnson. Jack Johnson's boxing career was over but he remained a popular figure especially with African American audiences. After appearing in Andlauer's *As the World Rolls On*, the former champ was once again bitten by the acting bug. He went on to appear in *For His Mother's Sake* (1922), produced by Blackburn Velde and *The Black Thunderbolt* (1922), producer unknown.

Besides New York, Chicago, Kansas City, and Jacksonville, the state of Texas was another oasis of black filmmaking. In San Antonio, Lone Star Pictures made several films including *Stranger From Way Out Yonder* (1922-3), *The Wrong Mr. Johnson* (1922-3) and *You Can't Keep A Good Man Down* (1922-3). Based in Dallas, the white-owned M. W. Baccus Films Company contributed *From Cotton Patch To Congress* (1922). These films are presumed lost; all that remains are the titles. Even less remains of Superior Art Productions of Houston and Cotton Blossom Productions, which were also active in Texas in the early 1920s and contributed to the vibrant regional film community but whose work has been covered by the sands of time.

DIXIE THEATRE
Present
A BIG SPECIAL FEATURE
The Sensation of the Year
TWO DAYS ONLY.
Saturday and Sunday, May 20 and 21
SEE
JACK JOHNSON
Ex-Heavyweight Champion of the World in Action
"For His Mother's Sake"

A blending of sobs and laughter, the love of a son who shouldered hardships and misfortune for love of his mother.

The last two rounds of the big bout in Mexico City has the spectators on their feet throughout. The round prior to the last sees Jack accepting a severe beating at the hands of the aggressive Lopez. Returning to his corner a badly beaten and dejected man he falls to thinking of home, his mother and brother's misstep for which he had taken the blame. All his plans seemed further away than ever at that minute. Coming out of his corner for the last round, Lopez finds himself facing a different Jack than in the previous round. After a minute of furious fighting, in which Jack proves the aggressor, the crowd sees Lopez sink to the floor from a terrific blow to the jaw and take the count.

See the Knockout in the Fifth Round. A picture all will want to see and other attractions.
DON'T MISS IT.

Sources

Torriano Berry, Venise T. Berry, The 50 Most Influential Black Films: A Celebration of African-American Talent, Determination and Creativity (New York: Citadel Press, 2001).

Eleanor Blau, "With Dignity: Films by Blacks for Blacks" in *The New York Times*, October 22, 1990.

Donald Bogle, Blacks in American Films and Television: an Encyclopedia (New York: Simon & Schuster, 1988).

Vincent Canby, "*Scar of Shame*, a Pioneer Black Film at Whitney" in The *New York Times*, March 18, 1976.

Thomas Cripps, Slow Fade to Black: The Negro in American Film 1900-1942 (New York: Oxford University Press, 1977).

Alan Gevinson, ed., Within Our Gates: Ethnicity in American Feature Films, 1911-1960 (Berkeley: University of California Press, 1997).

G. William Jones, Black Treasures: Lost and Found (Denton: University of North Texas, 1991).

G. Betty Kaplan Gubert, Miriam Sawyer, Caroline M. Fannin, Distinguished African Americans in Aviation and Space Science (Westport: The Oryx Press, 2002).

Phyllis R. Klotman and Gloria J. Gibson, Frame By Frame II: A Filmography of the African American Image (Bloomington: Indiana University Press, 1997).

J. A. Mangan and Andrew Ritchie (eds.), Ethnicity, Sport, Identity: Struggles for Status (Great Britain: Routeledge, 2005).

Barbara Tepa Lupack, Literary Adaptations in Black American Cinema: From Micheaux to Toni Morrison (Rochester: University of Rochester Press, 2002.

Christina Petersen, "The 'Reol' Story: Race Authorship and Consciousness in Robert Levy's Reol Productions, 1921-1926" in *Highbeam Business*, July 1, 2008.

Kansas City Museum at http://www.kansascitymuseum.org/

Metro Jacksonville's Distinguish Jacksonville: The Silent Film Industry at http://www.metrojacksonville.com

Norman Studios at http://www.normanstudios.org

Texas Historical Association at http://www.tshaonline.org

5

Oscar Micheaux: the Leading Man of Race Film

The biggest name in the production of race films was Oscar Micheaux. More than any other filmmaker, Micheaux showed a lifelong dedication to crafting stories of the African American experience. A driven write-director-producer, Micheaux can be also seen as Godfather of the independent film movement that made self-financed movies outside of the Hollywood system.

The child of former slaves, Micheaux (1884-1951) migrated to the booming city of Chicago in 1900. He worked as a Pullman Porter and saved enough money to buy a homestead in South Dakota by 1904.

Micheaux worked the land, built his own house, and began writing stories celebrating self-reliance for African American readers. He self-published *The Conquest* (1913) and *The Forged Note* (1915). After penning a third novel, *The Homesteader* (1917), the Johnson brothers of the Lincoln Motion Picture Company took notice.

George and Noble Johnson had been leading race filmmakers since 1916. For the producers of *The Realization of a Negro's Ambition* (1916) and *The Trooper of Company K* (1917), Micheaux's story of a self-made man seen in *The Homesteader* seemed like a solid fit. But once the producers began talking money with Micheaux, the self-made man himself had a different idea. Instead of taking a cut of the profits from Lincoln's production, Micheaux felt he could make the film himself. In 1918 he opened the Micheaux Film and Book Company and began crowd-funding investments. He quickly raised the money needed to produce his first film. *The Homesteader* (1919) premiered in Chicago and *The Defender* praised it as greatest race film of all time.

With this encouragement, Micheaux embarked on a new phase of his career. He had the skill to raise money, the talent to write and direct, and the determination to drive the chitlin' circuit and self-distribute his pictures. Micheaux was incredibly prolific, turning out racially-flavored melodramas such as *Within Our Gates* (1920), *The Symbol of the Unconquered* (1920), and *Birthright* (1924). Micheaux's movie machine emulated Hollywood by promoting his own version of screen stars promoting Lorenzo Tucker as the "colored Valentino," Ethel Moses as the "black Harlow," and Bee Freeman as the "sepia Mae West." Without a doubt, Micheaux's greatest film discovery was Paul Robeson, who made his screen debut in *Body and Soul* (1925).

Micheaux proved himself as race film's most reliable brand name. He continuously had new films in the pipeline, releasing nearly 50 films by 1948. Always ready to give the people what they want, Micheaux would remake popular titles into new films. The Micheaux operation was dealt a hard blow by the Depression and the coming of sound technology. But unlike many small race film producers that were pushed to the limit, Micheaux Productions made the transition to talkies. In 1931, he produced the first all-black produced sound film, *The Exile* (1931).

The Micheaux star factory included (clockwise from above left) Lorenzo "the colored Valentino" Tucker, Bee "the sepia Mae West" Freeman and Evelyn Preer.

If Micheaux's silent films were a response to racist elements in mainstream filmmaking and carried the message of self-reliance, the director's films of the early sound era aimed to be crowd-pleasing pot-boilers. Micheaux's talkies attracted audiences with exciting titles such as *Ten Minutes to Live* (1932), *Murder in Harlem* (1935), and *Underworld* (1936).

After releasing *Birthright* (1939), the Micheaux film factory slowed. Ten years later he released his final film, *The Betrayal* (1948). Within two years of Micheaux's last picture, Sidney Poitier entered the mainstream scene and the era of race films that Micheaux had defined was over. But even as the curtain came down on Micheaux Productions, the filmmaker made history. On June 28, his final film was reviewed by *The New York Times*: "Just for the record…*The Betrayal*, first all-Negro motion picture to have a Broadway premiere, now is being shown twice daily on a reserved-seat basis at the Mansfield Theatre. As the author, director, and

producer, Oscar Micheaux set his sights high, tackling a purpose-
ful and multifarious theme which requires slightly more than three
hours to expound.   The story…detail[s] the marital woes of an
enterprising young Negro who develops an agricultural empire in

South Dakota.   The film also contemplates…the relationship
between negroes and whites as members of the community as
well as partners in marriage." Operating independently from the
Hollywood movie factory, Micheaux's tireless work helped race
films to become noted and reviewed by the mainstream media.

Micheaux's work sometimes suffered from poor technical quality but his stories pushed audiences to think and consider difficult issues of race and acceptance. As the most prolific filmmaker of race films, Oscar Micheaux wrote his own legacy and remains the leading producer of race films and an artist that provided inspiration and entertainment to audiences overlooked by Hollywood.

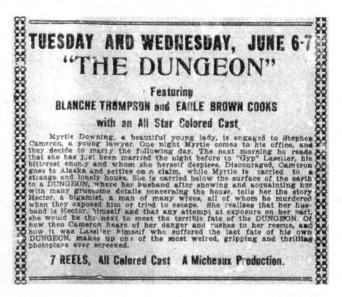

TUESDAY AND WEDNESDAY, JUNE 6-7
"THE DUNGEON"
Featuring
BLANCHE THOMPSON and EARLE BROWN COOKS
with an All Star Colored Cast

Myrtle Downing, a beautiful young lady, is engaged to Stephen Cameron, a young lawyer. One night Myrtle comes to his office, and they decide to marry the following day. The next morning he reads that she has just been married the night before to "Gyp" Lassiter, his bitterest enemy and whom she herself despises. Discouraged, Cameron goes to Alaska and settles on a claim, while Myrtle is carried to a strange and lonely house. She is carried below the surface of the earth to a DUNGEON, where her husband after showing and acquainting her with many gruesome details concerning the house, tells her the story. Hector, a bigamist, a man of many wives, all of whom he murdered when they exposed him or tried to escape. She realizes that her husband is Hector, himself and that any attempt at exposure on her part, she would be the next to meet the terrible fate of the DUNGEON. Of how then Cameron hears of her danger and rushes to her rescue, and how it was Lassiter himself who suffered the last fate of his own DUNGEON, makes up one of the most weird, gripping and thrilling photoplays ever screened.

7 REELS, All Colored Cast   A Micheaux Production.

Sources

"*The Betrayal* First All-Negro Film at Mansfield" in *The New York Times*, June 26, 1948.

Todd Boyd, ed., African Americans and Popular Culture (Westport: Praeger Press, 2008).

Michael Corcoran, Arnie Bernstein, Hollywood on Lake Michigan: 100+ Years of Chicago and the Movies (Chicago: Chicago Review Press, 2013).

Jeremy Geltzer, Oscar Micheaux: A Self-Made Man (Los Angeles: The Hollywood Press, 2013).

Patrick McGilligan, Oscar Micheaux: The Great and Only (New York: Harper Perennial, 2007).

Capturing a slice of life, Oscar Micheaux's motion pictures explored different types of relationships in the African American community seen in (clockwise): *Murder in Harlem* (1935), *Swing!* (1938), *The Exile* (1931), and *Veiled Aristocrats* (1932).

Veiled Aristocrats (1932)

Paul Robeson made his film debut opposite
Julia Theresa Russell in *Body and Soul* (1925).

Swing (1938)

"SWING!"

From the story "MANDY"
With CORA GREEN

In *Swing!* (1938), Eloise (Hazel Diaz) moves from Birmingham, Alabama to Harlem where she finds work in a cotton club.

Clockwise from above: *The Gunsaulus Mystery* (1921), *The Exile* (1931), and *God's Step-Children* (1938).

Oscar Micheaux's *The Wages of Sin* (1929), above, and *Underworld* (1936), below.

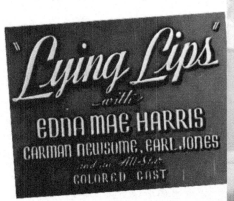

Edna Mae Harris stripped down for a sexy sequence in *Lying Lips* (1939). The following year she appeared in *The Notorious Elinor Lee* (1940) for Micheaux, which was his penultimate film.

God's Step Children (1938)

Birthright (1939)

The end of an era: Oscar Micheaux's final two motion pictures, *The Notorious Elinor Lee* (1940), above and *The Betrayal* (1948), right.

Oscar Micheaux

6

Spencer Williams and the Struggle with Sound

The coming of sound pictures changed everything. Within two years of the transition to talkies, many race filmmakers operating around the country vanished. Making movies was no longer as cheap and easy with the new technology.

One producer had been through drastic changes before. Al Christie began his film career in 1909. He was sent west in 1911 and opened the very first studio located in Hollywood. When Universal Pictures acquired the independent studio he worked for, Christie left and opened his own. By 1916, the Christie Film Company began producing short low budget pictures. In 1929, filling the void left by the race filmmakers either bankrupted by the Great Depression or unable to navigate the conversion to sound, Christie began making all-black talkies.

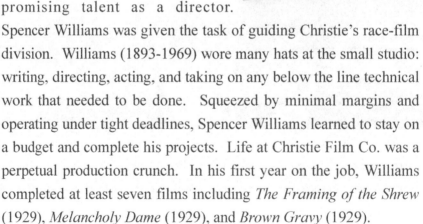

Christie hired a production assistant but quickly saw the young man's promising talent as a director. Spencer Williams was given the task of guiding Christie's race-film division. Williams (1893-1969) wore many hats at the small studio: writing, directing, acting, and taking on any below the line technical work that needed to be done. Squeezed by minimal margins and operating under tight deadlines, Spencer Williams learned to stay on a budget and complete his projects. Life at Christie Film Co. was a perpetual production crunch. In his first year on the job, Williams completed at least seven films including *The Framing of the Shrew* (1929), *Melancholy Dame* (1929), and *Brown Gravy* (1929).

The Blood of Jesus (1941)

Meanwhile, a white Texas-based motion pictures producer named Alfred N. Sack incorporated Sack Amusement Enterprises in the late 1920s. Soon he was presenting race films such as *Harlem is Heaven* (1932) with dancing legend Bill Robinson, *Bubbling Over* (1934) with singing star Ethel Waters, and *Dark Manhattan* (1937) with suave leading man Ralph Cooper.

After Christie Film closed its shop in 1933, Sack hired Spencer Williams. At Sack, Williams acted in Herb Jeffries'

popular Western series but he was also given the freedom to direct personal projects. Sack's studio allowed Williams the opportunity to make the films that he is best remembered for: *Blood of Jesus* (1941), *Go Down Death!* (1944), *Dirty Gertie from Harlem U.S.A.* (1946), and *Juke Joint* (1947).

Spencer Williams made his directorial debut with *The Blood of Jesus* (1941)

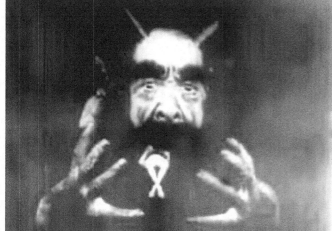

After living a criminal high life, Big Jim (Spencer Williams) experiences visions of Hell in the Sack production of *Go Down Death!* (1944).

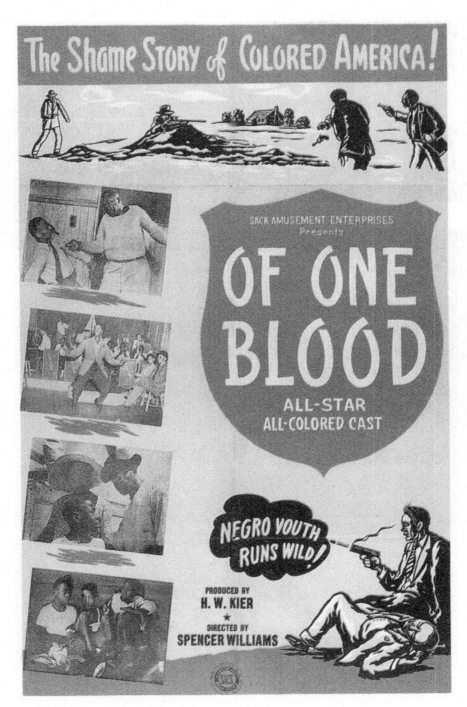

Of One Blood (1944)

Directed by Spencer Williams: (Clockwise from top) *Juke Joint* (1947), *Marching On!* (1943), and *The Girl in Room 20* (1946)

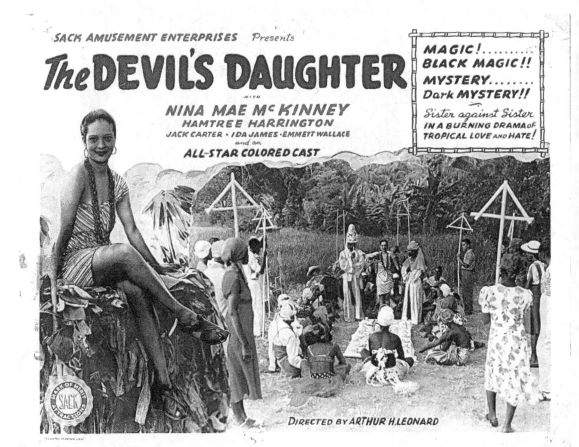

The Devil's Daughter (1939)

By the 1950s as the era of race films faded, Spencer Williams became known to white audiences for his work on television, starring as Amos in 78 episodes of *The Amos 'n Andy Show* (1950-1955).

Williams rose through the ranks at an independent Hollywood studio before making his own spiritually-flavored films. As the opportunity to produce race films became scarce, Williams transitioned to mainstream entertainment for a successful career, even if it lacked the heart and soul he gave to his own movies. Many Sack-Williams films have been recovered and restored by the Southwest Film-Video Archives in Dallas allowing this great legacy to survive.

Spencer Williams as his alter ego, Andy Brown

Sources

Spencer Moon, Reel Black Talk: A Sourcebook of 50 American Filmmakers
        (Westport: Greenwood Press, 1997).

Judith Weisenfeld, Hollywood Be Thy Name: African American Religion in
        American Film, 1929-1949 (Berkeley: University of California Press, 2007).

"Spencer Williams Jr. Who Played Andy in *Amos 'n' Andy* TV Series" in *The New
        York Times*, December 24, 1969.

7

Black Cowboys & Showtime at the Apollo

From singing cowboys to swinging jazz ensembles, the race films showcased a wide range of talent. One thing these diverse films had in common was the celebration of African American heroes. As black filmmakers became more sophisticated, their celebration of courage reached an international stage.

Herb Jeffries was discovered at the 1933 Chicago World's Fair fronting the Earl Hines Orchestra. Jeffries (1913-2014) embodied a certain swinging coolness. By 1940 he was singing with Duke Ellington's band. Squeezed into his busy touring schedule Jeffries starred in a series of all-black musical westerns produced by Sack Amusements. These were race film's answer to Gene Autry and Roy Rogers: *Two Gun Man from Harlem* (1938), *Harlem Rides the Range* (1939), and the picture that would give Jeffries his onscreen nickname, *The Bronze Buckeroo* (1939). Jeffries wasn't the first black cowboy, that would be Bill Pickett, but Jeffries' easygoing style make him popular with black audiences.

Richard C. Kahn directed Herb
Jeffries' trilogy of westerns: *Two
Gun-Man from Harlem* (1938), *The
Bronze Buckeroo* (1939), and
Harlem Rides the Range (1939).
Harlem Rides the Ranges offered
suave songs, action packed gun-
fights and desolate landscapes.
The film was written by Spencer
Williams, who also appeared as the
sheriff, above, in black hat.

ALL-NEGRO WESTERN

ALFRED N. SACK Presents

HERBERT JEFFREY

— IN —

BRONZE BUCKAROO

— WITH —

SPENCER WILLIAMS
CLARENCE BROOKS

and the

FOUR TONES

Distributed by SACK AMUSEMENT ENTERPRISES

directed by
RICHARD C. KAHN

With bar room brawls, a swinging single, "I've Got the Pay Day Blues," and an evil rancher played by Spencer Williams, *The Bronze Buckaroo* (1939) was the best black western.

"The can't hang you any higher for two murders."

Calypso Joe (1957)

In 1935, Ralph Cooper hit the stage as the first MC of Amateur Night at the Apollo Theater in Harlem. Two years later he formed Million Dollar Productions backed by white producer-brothers Harry and Leo Popkin. Cooper (1908-1992) wrote and starred in the film noir-ish *Gangsters on the Loose* (1937), *The Duke Is Tops* (1938), and *Gang War* (1940).

Cooper's partner, Leo Popkin (1914-2011), directed several comedy-thriller race films such as *Gang Smashers* (1938), *Reform School* (1939), and *One Dark Night* (1939). Million Dollar also crafted vehicles around African American sports stars, showcasing Joe Louis in the biographical short *The Brown Bomber* (1939)

and football star Kenny Washington in *While Thousands Cheer* (1940). One commentator observed that while Oscar Micheaux might have been the most prolific race filmmaker, Million Dollar Productions made films more accessible to mixed race audiences as mainstream entertainment than any other black production company.

On the Apollo's storied stage Ralph Cooper frequently introduced one of the theater's mainstay comedians: Dewey 'Pigmeat' Markham. Pigmeat had created his character in traveling burlesque shows during the 1920s. By the time he hit the Harlem stage, his courtroom routine was a classic.

Dressed in black robes and making an entrance with the catchphrase "heyeah come da judge," Pigmeat would arbitrate on comic criminals and pass down absurd judgments. Markham appeared in a series of films made for race film producer Toddy Pictures including *Am I Guilty?* (1940), *Mr. Smith Goes Ghost* (1940), *Fight That Ghost* (1946), and *House-Rent Party* (1946). Pigmeat's syncopated musical-comedy style was distinctive; he pioneered urban comedy and cut a recording in 1968 that has been called the first rap record.

Besides Pigmeat Markham, during the 1940s Toddy Pictures added other African American talents to its roster, including Ralph Cooper. The small studio was run by Ted Toddy, a Hollywood veteran who had worked at Universal and Columbia. In 1940 Toddy established an independent race film shingle based in Atlanta and picked up distribution for other producers. Toddy packaged pictures with the most recognizable African American performers including Mantan Moreland in *Professor Creeps* (1942) and Eddie Green in *Eddie Green's Laff Jamboree* (1945).

By the end of the decade, Toddy released several musical shorts that captured the spirit of the jazz age: *Harlem Mood, Harlem Dynamite, Harlem Jam Session,* and *Harlem After Midnight* (all 1949).

One of Toddy's more serious pictures was *Fighting Americans* (1944), which offered viewers a look at the Tuskegee airmen in training. Capturing a similar historical perspective, William D. Alexander (1916-1991) formed the Associated Producers of Negro Pictures. After producing jazz shorts and race films, such as *Rhythm in a Riff* (1946), *Jivin' in Be-Bop* (1947), and *Souls in Sin* (1949), Alexander focused his camera on current events affecting the black community. In a series of shorts called *The By-Line Newsreels* (1953-1956), Alexander interviewed black government officials and leading political figures.

Leo Popkin's *While Thousands Cheer* (1940)

Spirit of Youth (1938)

House-Rent Party (1946)

Fight That Ghost (1946)

Alexander's political activism increased. He left the U.S. to produce a series of documentaries that chronicled the challenges and triumphs of emerging states in Africa. A world away from American race films, Alexander's *Village of Hope* (1964), the story of a Liberian leper colony, won the Short Film *Palme d'Or* at Cannes. *Portrait of Ethiopia* (1965) was honored at the Venice Film Festival. *Wealth in Wood* (1967) also shot in Liberia, was recognized with a bronze medal at Madrid's

International Film Festival. While black filmmakers sought to uplift

African American audiences, Alexander took his work to the world's stage.

Sources

"Ralph Cooper, Who Found Stars At Apollo's Amateur Nights, Dies" in *The New York Times*, August 6, 1992

"William Alexander, Producer Featuring Blacks, Dies at 75" in *The New York Times*, December 6, 1991.

AFI Catalog of Motion Pictures Produced in the United States (Berkeley: University of California Press, 1997).

Tino Balio, Grand Design: Hollywood as a Modern Business Enterprise, 1930-1939 (Berkeley: University of California Press, 1996).

Spencer Moon, Reel Black Talk: A Sourcebook of 50 American Filmmakers (Westport: Greenwood Press, 1997).

William Yardley, "Herb Jeffries, 'Bronze Buckaroo' of Song and Screen, Dies at 100 (or So)" in *The New York Times*, May 26, 2014.

8

Music and Comedy

Hollywood studio executives had to learn how to manufacture movie stars. By contrast, race films teemed with talents that had honed their acts in vaudeville, burlesque, and traveling medicine show troupes. Ford "Buck" Washington and John "Bubbles" Sublett teamed together in the 1920s. When Radio City Music Hall opened in 1932 Buck & Bubbles were the first black artists to take the stage.

Buck hammered tunes on piano while Bubbles stamped out a dance routine. New York-based Monte Brice Productions made several short films that captured the rhythmic routine of Buck & Bubbles in *Black Narcissus* (1929), *Fowl Play* (1929), and *Darktown Follies* (1930). Buck & Bubbles's reputation grew. Hollywood's top hoofer, Fred Astaire, considered Bubbles the greatest tap dancer he'd ever seen. Warner Bros. called on the performers for *Varsity Show* (1937). MGM even wrote special showcases for Bubbles in *Cabin in the Sky* (1943) and *I Dood It* (1943).

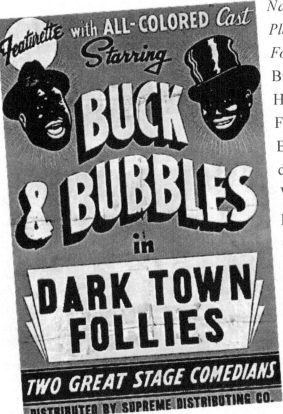

While Buck & Bubbles were working Radio City in midtown Manhattan, two talented women were burning up the stages on separate continents. Both rose from rural poverty to reach international success: Josephine Baker and Ethel Waters.

Josephine Baker left East St. Louis for the Harlem club scene but she really came alive when she took her act to Paris. The exotic performer headlined mind-blowing, eye popping, sexy shows along the Champs d'Elysees and road-showed throughout Europe and Northern Africa. Her striptease act was far too hot for America so her films were mostly seen in overseas: *Siren of the Tropics* (1927), *Die Frauen von Folies Bergères* (1927), *La revue des revues* (1927), *La folie du jour* (1929), *Zouzou* (1934), and *Princess Tam Tam* (1935).

Josephine Baker in
Princess Tam Tam
(1935), left

Baker danced the Charleston
in *Die Frauen von Folies
Bergères* (1927), right

Baker in *Zou Zou*
(1934), left

Keeping her clothes on, Ethel Waters commanded attention with her brassy personality and powerful voice. Waters spring-boarded from a star performer during the Harlem Renaissance to become a

recording artist at Columbia in the 1920s. She introduced soon-to-be-standard tunes: "Sweet Georgia Brown," "Heebie Jeebies," and "Stormy Weather." Vitaphone's East Coast studio cast Waters in a featurette entitled *Rufus Jones for President* (1933), where she introduced a promising 8-year old actor named Sammy Davis Jr. Ten years later, Waters was still at the top of her career. MGM signed her to star in *Cabin in the Sky* (1943). Six years after *Cabin* when she played a decidedly unglamorous laundress in *Pinky* (1949), Waters was nominated for an Academy Award. In the 1950s Waters took over the title role in the TV series *Beulah*. It was only in the 1960s after over 40 years in showbiz did the powerhouse that was Ethel Waters begin to slow down.

Another performer with incredible unstoppable energy was Cab Calloway. Usually attired in a stylish zoot suit, Calloway's supersized personality entertained audiences at New York's famed Cotton Club. By 1931 he was known for his signature song "Minnie the Moocher." The Fleischer brothers saw Calloway's act as ripe for an animated adaptation and placed his songs in several Betty Boop shorts including *Minnie the Moocher* (1932) and *The Old Man of the Mountain* (1933). Paramount Pictures built a film around his act: *Cab Calloway's Hi-De-Ho* (1934). Forty years after his first Hi-De-Hos Calloway would once again charm audiences with

the call and response of his Minnie the Moocher routine in *The Blues Brothers* (1980).

Calloway may have been the Hi-De-Ho Man but his contemporary Louis Jordan became known as the King of the Jukebox for his swinging numbers. Jordan was suave, stylish, and funny. He was able to crossover and appeal to white audiences especially when "Is You Is Or Is You Ain't My Baby" hit #1 on the pop charts in 1944. After appearing in Universal's all-star *Follow the Boys* (1944), Jordan rode out the swing craze in race films like *Beware* (1946) and *Reet, Petite and Gone* (1947).

By 1947 the swing film craze was fading and race pictures were in their final years. A Kansas City filmmaker named Josh Binney formed All American Pictures and captured the final years of great music on film. After directing Cab Calloway in *Hi-De-Ho*, Binney went on to make *Killer Diller* (1948) , *Boarding House Blues* (1948), and *The Joint is Jumpin'* (1949). *Boarding House* featured a comedienne who would soon be known as the Funniest Woman in the World: Moms Mabley. Mabley's act continued on stage as race films were replaced by a new generation of pop culture icons. Hollywood began to strategically incorporate African American talent mainstream movies undercutting the uniqueness of race films and diluting the market for all-black motion pictures. It was clear by 1949 that an era was ending.

ALL AMERICAN PICTURES

Presents

Dusty FLETCHER

in

"BOARDING HOUSE BLUES"

with

• LUCKY MILLINDER & BAND
• BULL MOOSE JACKSON
• UNA MAE CARLISLE
• JOHN MASON
• BERRY BROTHERS
• JACKIE MABLEY
• STUMP & STUMPY
• LEWIS & WHITE

AND A
Brilliant
ALL COLORED CAST

Directed by
JOSH BINNEY

9

Hollywood Race Films

After leaving his brother in charge of the pioneering race-film studio, Lincoln Motion Picture Company, Noble Johnson joined Universal Pictures as their on-staff exotic player. Noble played cannibal kings, Indian chiefs, savages, and slaves. Between 1917-1950 Noble Johnson accumulated over 150 credits but never a leading role. He was not alone.

Rex Ingram's acting career began in 1918 when he played uncredited natives in First National's *Tarzan of the Apes* (1918) and Fox's *Salome* (1918). Roles were limited for a black actor in Hollywood but Ingram was called to appear in films such as *The Ten Commandments* (1923) and *King of Kings* (1927). He later turned in star quality performances as Jim in *The Adventures of Huckleberry Finn* (1939) opposite Mickey Rooney and as the towering genie in *Thief of Bagdad* (1940).

By the late 1920s, the conversion to sound technology presented challenges to the entire film industry. Seemingly overnight singing and dancing films became incredibly popular. The year that *The Broadway Melody* (1929) claimed the Academy Award for Best Picture with toe-tapping Tin Pan Alley tunes, two other motion pictures that drew on African American performers presented a glimpse of black culture.

King Vidor had been a star filmmaker since directing *The Big Parade* (1925). At MGM he had the power and influence to convince Louis B. Mayer to green light an all-black musical to be shot on location in Tennessee and Arkansas with unknown actors. But even with Vidor's influence, the studio felt the project was so risky that the director was pressured to pitch in his own salary to make *Hallelujah!* (1929). The film's production was equally challenging. *Hallelujah!* was Vidor's first talkie and, at the time, very few studio films had been shot on location off the sealed soundstages of Hollywood. But the gamble paid off. *Hallelujah!* was a powerful document and Vidor was nominated for an Academy Award. While the film was commercially and critically successful, it did not immediately lead to more opportunities at MGM for black actors.

A few months before *Hallelujah!* Fox Film Corp. released *Hearts in Dixie* (1929). *Dixie* was an all-black musical film that featured a stately actor named Clarence Muse (1889-1979). Muse cut his

teeth during the Harlem Renaissance. Once he hit Hollywood he commenced a five-decade career that would include 150+ films. In *Dixie*, Muse played the wise patriarch of his family. More problematic was the actor who played Muse's son-in-law, a man named Lincoln Theodore Monroe Andrew Perry. Perry performed under a stage name that has become symbolic of racial stereotype: Stepin Fetchit, the self-proclaimed "Laziest Man in the World."

Fetchit created his act on the vaudeville stage as a lazy, ignorant, shuffling character. He combined all the negative qualities of a racist caricature for the entertainment of white folks. Beginning in 1925, Fetchit brought his character to movie screens providing comic relief. But he was incredibly popular. In its review of *Hearts in Dixie*, *The New York Times* wrote that Fetchit "who impersonates a sluggard named Gummy is a remarkable comedian." Despite poor taste, Fetchit's act also proved financially successful—earning him over $1 million. Also notable, Fetchit was the first black actor to receive screen credit in a studio film. Despite his achievements, history has not been kind. Fetchit has become a symbol of America's painfully racist attitudes and demeaning roles available to black actors.

Hollywood's studios showed second burst of interest in African American actors a few years later. Universal paired Claudette Colbert with Louise Beavers in *Imitation of Life* (1934). MGM tapped the talents of Paul Robeson and Hattie McDaniel for *Show Boat* (1936). Warners assembled an all-black all-star cast for *The Green Pastures* (1936). Fox cast the Dandridge Sisters as a specialty act in *The Big Broadcast of 1936*.

Paul Robeson had an incredibly versatile career before appearing on film. He earned a law degree from Columbia University; sang gospel uptown in

The Emperor Jones (1933)

Harlem and performed in Eugene O'Neill's plays in mid-town Manhattan. Robeson was drafted by the NFL to play for the Akron Pros and later gave public voice to his leftwing political views. Robeson was a rare talent. Oscar Micheaux signed Robeson up to play a corrupt and charismatic preacher in

Body and Soul (1925). After working for Micheaux, Robeson took the lead in the film adaptation of O'Neill's *Emperor Jones* (1933) and appeared in a British picture entitled *The Song of Freedom* (1936).

MGM took notice of Robeson's great talent. Composer Oscar Hammerstein II and lyricist Jerome Kern expanded the role of Joe in *Show Boat* for Robeson—the performer's delivery of "Ol' Man River" would become definitive. Robeson performed the role on the London stage in 1928 and on Broadway in 1932. The studio never even considered anyone else for the role in the 1936 film adaptation: Joe was made for Robeson's booming baritone and colossal physique.

That same year Warner Bros. offered a swinging biblical adaptation called *The Green Pastures*. Like *Show Boat*, *Pastures* also began as an award winning stage production. Marc Connelly won a Pulitzer Prize for the play. For the film adaptation, Rex Ingram was transformed into "De Lawd" with a powdered white beard. Oscar Polk played the angel Gabriel. Eddie Anderson became Noah. *The Green Pastures* romped through the Book of Genesis adapted as an African American folktale.

A few years later Arthur Freed, a powerful producer in MGM's musical division, called together a very similar cast for *Cabin in the Sky* (1943). This time Ingram played Lucifer with Louis Armstrong

and Mantan Moreland among his devilish minions. They faced off against Oscar Polk, who played a righteous deacon. In *Cabin in the Sky*, Eddie Anderson was the central figure as Little Joe Jackson. Little Joe is decent man, torn and tormented by higher powers. He's tempted by demonic forces—in the stunning figure of Lena Horne as Sweet Georgia Brown—to forsake his god-fearing wife Petunia (Ethel Waters). After briefly succumbing to temptation—and who wouldn't when faced with Lena Horne—Little Joe chooses the high road. *Cabin* was the first film credit for Vincente Minnelli, who would soon to become Hollywood's top musical director.

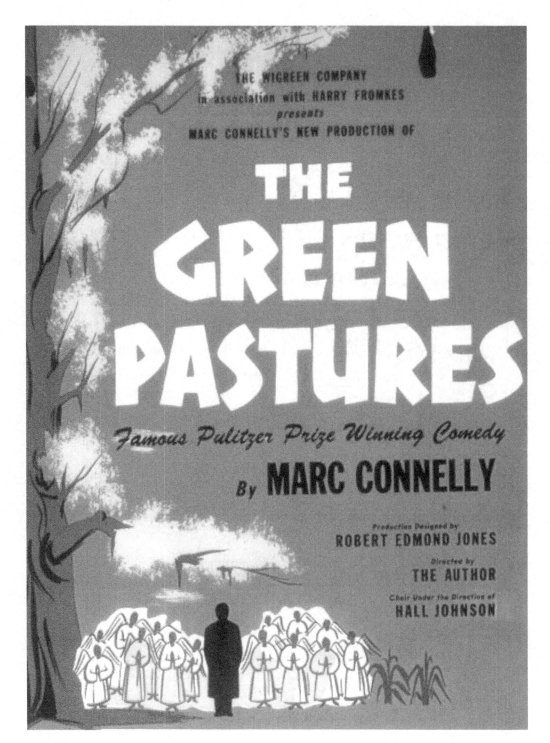

Only a few months after *Cabin in the Sky*, Fox released *Stormy Weather* (1943). *Stormy Weather* showcased top African American performers: Lena Horne sang and Bill Robinson tap danced. The ensemble included swinging performances by Cab Calloway, Fats Waller, and the acrobatic dance duo the Nicholas brothers, Fayard and Harold. Three years later Walt Disney made his own tribute to African American culture with *Song of the South* (1946). Disney cast James Baskett, an actor who had only previously appeared in race films such as *Harlem is Heaven* (1932) and *Gone Harlem* (1938). The mouse house transformed Baskett into a cuddly kid friendly Uncle Remus who introduced "Zip-a-dee-doo-dah." The number won an Academy Award for Best Song and Baskett was awarded an honorary Oscar.

Despite specialty performances in all-star musicals, there were few roles available to black performers in mainstream movies. James Baskett was the second African American talent to be recognized by Hollywood. The first, Hattie McDaniel, had earned a Best Supporting Actress Academy Award five years earlier as Mammie in *Gone with the Wind* (1939). McDaniel was a memorable performer but even she could only find film work as domestic help. McDaniel served Hollywood's greatest stars—Marlene Dietrich in *Blonde Venus (*1932), Mae West in *I'm No Angel* (1933), Jean Harlow in *China Seas* (1935), Katharine Hepburn in *Alice Adams* (1935), Shirley Temple in *The Little Colonel* (1935), Barbara Stanwyck in *Stella Dallas* (1937), Carole Lombarde in *Nothing Sacred* (1937), and Ginger Rogers in *Vivacious Lady* (1938). But no leading roles were available for McDaniel.

Other actresses, such as Louise Beavers, Butterfly McQueen and Juanita Moore were stuck in similar domestic roles. Dooley Wilson performed Sam's favorite song in *Casablanca* (1942) but he was basically domestic help. After a decade of playing assorted bellhops, chauffeurs, and door-

© TODDY PICTURES COMPANY

men, Eddie Anderson found steady employment as Jack Benny's wisecracking right hand man Rochester on radio and TV from 1937-1965.

The most memorable man-servant during the 1930s and 1940s was Mantan Moreland. Mantan has been sidelined by history. He has been seen as per-former who profited from black stereotypes with a pop-eyed expression and signature line: "Feets do your stuff!" The real man was more interesting. Mantan began as a vaudeville comic until he took a bit role in *The Green Pastures*. From there he found work in race movies—he made a memorable sidekick to cowboy Herb Jeffries in *Harlem on the Prairie* (1937), boxer Joe Louis in *Spirit of Youth* (1938), and football star Kenny Washington in *While Thousands Cheer* (1940). Soon Mantan was headlining his own comedy films for Dixie National Pictures: *Mr. Washington Goes to Town* (1941),

Up Jumped the Devil (1941)

Lucky Ghost (1942)

Lucky Ghost (1942)

Professor Creeps (1942)

Professor Creeps (1942)

Tall, Tan and Terrific (1946)

Mantan Messes Up (1946)

The Return of Mandy's Husband (1948)

Come On, Cowboy! (1948)

Mantan Moreland was one of the few actors who was able to move between race films and mainstream Hollywood. His scaredy-cat expression was suited to b-movie antics. Poverty Row studio Monogram Pictures contracted Moreland for cheapie thrillers such as *Drums of the Desert* (1940), *King of the Zombies* (1941), and *Phantom Killer* (1942). The studio soon found Moreland the perfect partner, teaming him with Sidney Toler in the Charlie Chan series. Toler played the sagacious Asian sleuth while Moreland remained on edge as Birmingham Brown, assistant and occasional chauffeur. Toler and Moreland furiously churned out programmers through the 1940s: *Charlie Chan in the Secret Service* (1944), *Charlie Chan in the Chinese Cat* (1944), *Black Magic* (1944), *The Jade Mask* (1945), *The Scarlet Clue* (1945), *The Shanghai Cobra* (1945), *Dark Alibi* (1946), *The Trap* (1946), and *Shadows Over Chinatown* (1946).

When a new actor stepped into the Chan character, Mantan stayed on for six more pictures including *The Chinese Ring* (1947), *The Golden Eye* (1948), and *The Sky Dragon* (1949). These films, popular at the time, are now seen as racist relics with Mantan's frightened act and non-Asian actors in make up.

Mantan Moreland was versatile; he was able to transition from race films to mainstream b-movies. He just as easily jumped from lowbrow slapstick to high-brow drama—in the 1950s he was considered by Moe Howard as a possible replacement for Shemp as the third stooge. Moreland also played Estragon in an all-black version of *Waiting for Godot* on Broadway directed by Herbert Berghof in 1957. Political correctness aside, Mantan Moreland was a fun and fascinating performer that deserves to be remembered.

By the late 1940s Hollywood filmmakers began to show a greater interest in presenting realistic portrayals of the African American experience. Within a single year four studio films were released that focused on race issues. Fox's *Pinky* (1949) followed a light skinned black girl who passed for white in the North as she returned to her Southern home to find a racially divided town. *Lost Boundaries* (1949) focused on a young black doctor forced to pass himself off as white. In a more typical Hollywood move, both *Pinky* and *Lost Boundaries* cast white actors (Jeanne Crain and Mel Ferrer) as the African American protagonists. MGM adapted William Faulkner's *Intruder in the*

Stanley Kramer produced *Home of the Brave* (1949), the first of the message films that would define his career.

Dust (1949) with Juano Hernandez in the lead as a curmudgeonly black man wrongly accused of murder. In the fourth race based studio picture released that year, Stanley Kramer, a filmmaker known for his social-issue films, looked at racism in the military ranks for *Home of the Brave* (1949).

Nineteen forty-nine was a peak mid-century period for race issues in film. The year after Hollywood made strides in confronting difficult issues, a newcomer made his screen debut. Sidney Poitier appeared in his first major film: *No Way Out* (1950). Poitier became Hollywood's first African American leading man. Within a decade he was nominated for an Academy Award and by 1964 he claimed the golden statuette for *Lilies of the Field* (1963). While Hollywood celebrated Poitier, another

figure was also breaking down race barriers. Jackie Robinson, the first black player to integrate Major League Baseball, starred in his own biopic: *The Jackie Robinson Story* (1950). Produced independently, *The Jackie Robinson Story* was released in the same year as Poitier's debut. Together these cultural icons helped move the racial dialogue forward.

Jackie Robinson and Sidney Poitier represented the first real steps toward the integration of African American talent into mainstream commercial films and popular culture. But their high profile pictures also signaled a death knell for race films. As Hollywood took steps toward integration, the race films of the separate cinema became a relic of a different era. By 1950 the era of race film production was over and soon forgotten. For decades these driven filmmakers and talented performers were overlooked by history until being rediscovered. By remembering the men and women who strived for recognition and equality in independent films, the American film industry can be seen with a new dimension.

Sources

"Hattie M'Daniel, Beulah of Radio" in *The New York Times*, October 27, 1952.

"Josephine Baker Is Dead in Paris at 68" in *The New York Times*, April 13, 1975.

"Moreland, Actor is Dead at 72" in *The New York Times*, September 29, 1973.

C. Gerald Fraser, "Dewy (Pigmeat) Markham, Vaudeville and TV Comedian" in *The New York Times*, December 16, 1981.

C. Gerald Fraser, "Ethel Waters Is Dead" in *The New York Times*, September 2, 1981.

Mordaunt Hall "Art in Negro Picture *Hearts in Dixie* Is an Outstanding Achievement in Dialogue and Singing" in *The New York Times*, March 10, 1929.

Mordaunt Hall, "Paul Robeson in the Pictorial Conception of Eugene O'Neill's Play, *The Emperor Jones*" in *The New York Times,* September 20, 1933.

Aljean Harmetz, "Lena Horne, Singer and Actress, Dies at 92" in *The New York Times*, May 10, 2010.

"*The Green Pastures* at Last Seen in Film at Music Hall—Rex Ingram as De Lawd" in *The New York Times*, July 17, 1936.

"*Cabin in the Sky*, a Musical Fantasy, With Ethel Waters, at Loew's Criterion"in *The New York Times,* May 28, 1943.

"What Blacks Thought of *Cabin in the Sky*" in *The New York Times,* February 2, 1983.

John S. Wilson, "Cab Calloway Is Dead at 86; 'Hi-de-hi-de-ho' Jazz Man" in *The New York Times,* November 20, 1994.

10

Recognition

From the 1920s through the 1960s Hollywood movies presented the world according to a white male voice. But through much effort, diverse talents began to emerge onscreen. African American performers and craftspeople broke through barriers and were soon recognized with Hollywood's highest achievements. These performers were celebrated not because they were African Americans, but because they were truly great talents.

Academy Award Winners for Best Actor in a Leading Role

Sidney Poitier, *Lilies of the Field* (1963)

Denzel Washington, *Training Day* (2001)

Jamie Foxx, *Ray* (2004)

Forest Whitaker, *The Last King of Scotland* (2006)

Academy Award Winners for Best Actress in a Leading Role

Halle Berry, *Monster's Ball* (2001)

Academy Award Winner for Best Writing (Adapted Screenplay)

Geoffrey Fletcher, *Precious* (2009)

John Ridley, *12 Years a Slave* (2013)

Academy Award Winners for Best Actor in a Supporting Role

Louis Gossett, Jr., *An Officer and a Gentleman* (1982)

Denzel Washington, *Glory* (1989)

Cuba Gooding, Jr., *Jerry Maguire* (1996)

Morgan Freeman, *Million Dollar Baby* (2004)

Academy Award Winners for Best Actress in a Supporting Role

Hattie MacDaniel, *Gone with the Wind* (1939)

Whoopie Goldberg, *Ghost* (1990)

Jennifer Hudson, *Dreamgirls* (2006)

Mo'Nique, *Precious* (2009)

Octavia Spencer, *The Help* (2011)

Lupita Nyong'o, *12 Years a Slave* (2013)

Academy Award Nominees for Best Actor in a Leading Role

Sidney Poitier, *The Defiant Ones* (1958)

James Earl Jones, *The Great White Hope* (1970)

Paul Winfield, *Sounder* (1972)

Dexter Gordon, *Round Midnight* (1986)

Laurence Fishburne, *What's Love Got to Do with It* (1993)

Morgan Freeman, *The Shawshank Redemption* (1994)

Denzel Washington, *The Hurricane* (1999)

Will Smith, *Ali* (2001)

Don Cheadle, *Hotel Rwanda* (2004)

Terence Howard, *Hustle & Flow* (2005)

Will Smith, *The Pursuit of Happyness* (2006)

Morgan Freeman, *Invictus* (2009)

Denzel Washington, *Flight* (2012)

Chiwetel Ejofor, *12 Years a Slave* (2013)

Academy Award Nominees for Best Actress in a Leading Role

Dorothy Dandridge, *Carmen Jones* (1954)

Diana Ross, *Lady Sings the Blues* (1972)

Cicely Tyson, *Sounder* (1972)

Diahann Carroll, *Claudine* (1974)

Whoopie Goldberg, *The Color Purple* (1985)

Angela Bassett, *What's Love Got to Do with It* (1993)

Gabourey Sidbe, *Precious* (2009)

Viola Davis, *The Help* (2011)

Quvenzhane Wallis, *Beasts of the Southern Wild* (2012)

Academy Award Nominees for Best Actor in a Supporting Role

Rupert Crosse, *The Reivers* (1969)

Howard Rollins, *Ragtime* (1981)

Adolph Caesar, *A Soldier's Story* (1984)

Morgan Freeman, *Street Smart* (1987)

Denzel Washington, *Cry Freedom* (1987)

Jaye Davidson, *The Crying Game* (1992)

Samuel L. Jackson, *Pulp Fiction* (1994)

Michael Clarke Duncan, *The Green Mile* (1999)

Djimon Hounsou, *In America* (2003)

Jamie Foxx, *Collateral* (2004)

Djimon Hounsou, *Blood Diamond* (2006)

Eddie Murphy, *Dreamgirls* (2006)

Barkhad Abdi, *Captain Phillips* (2013)

Academy Award Nominees for Best Actress in a Supporting Role

Ethel Waters, *Pinky* (1949)

Juanita Moore, *Imitation of Life* (1959)

Beah Richards, *Guess Who's Coming to Dinner* (1967)

Alfre Woodard, *Cross Creek* (1983)

Oprah Winfrey, *The Color Purple* (1985)

Marianne Jean-Baptiste, *Secrets & Lies* (1996)

Queen Latifah, *Chicago* (2002)

Sophie Okonedo, *Hotel Rwanda* (2004)

Ruby Dee, *American Gangster* (2007)

Viola Davis, *Doubt* (2008)

Taraji P. Henson, *The Curious Case of Benjamin Button* (2008)

Academy Award Nominees for Direction
John Singleton, *Boyz n the Hood* (1991)

Lee Daniels, *Precious* (2009)

Steve McQueen, *12 Years a Slave* (2013)

Academy Award Nominee for Cinematography
Remi Adefarasin, *Elizabeth* (1998)

Academy Award Nominee for Editing
Hugh A. Robertson, *Midnight Cowboy* (1969)

Academy Award Nominees for Writing (Original Screenplay)
Suzanne de Passe, *Lady Sings the Blues* (1972)

Spike Lee, *Do the Right Thing* (1989)

John Singleton, *Boyz n the Hood* (1991)

Academy Award Nominee for Writing (Adapted Screenplay)
Lonnie Elder, *Sounder* (1972)

Charles Fuller, *A Soldier's Story* (1984)

Academy Award Nominees for Costume Design
Ruth E. Carter, *Malcolm X* (1992)

Ruth E. Carter, *Amistad* (1997)

Sharen Davis, *Ray* (2004)

Sharen Davis, *Dreamgirls* (2006)

Academy Award Winners for Best Score

Prince, *Purple Rain* (1984)

Herbie Hancock, *Round Midnight* (1986)

Academy Award Nominees for Best Score

Duke Ellington, *Paris Blues* (1961)

Quincy Jones, *In Cold Blood* (1967)

Isaac Hayes, *Shaft* (1971)

Quincy Jones, *The Wiz* (1978)

Quincy Jones, Andrae Crouch & Caiphus Semenya, *The Color Purple* (1985)

Jonas Gwangwa, *Cry Freedom* (1987)

Academy Award Winners for Best Original Song

Isaac Hayes, "Theme from Shaft" from *Shaft* (1971)

Irene Cara, "Flashdance (What a Feeling)" from *Flashdance* (1983)

Stevie Wonder, "I Just Called to Say I Love You" from *The Woman in Red* (1984)

Lionel Ritchie, "Say You, Say Me" from *White Nights* (1985)

Juicy J, Frayser Boy and DJ Paul, "It's Hard Out Here for a Pimp" from *Hustle & Flow* (2005)

John Legend and Common, "Glory" from *Selma* (2014)

Academy Award Nominees for Original Song

Quincy Jones and Bob Russell, "The Eyes of Love" from *Banning* (1967)

Quincy Jones and Bob Russell, "For Love of Ivy" from *For Love of Ivy* (1968)

Lionel Ritchie, "Endless Love" from *Endless Love* (1981)

Ray Parker, Jr., "Ghostbusters" from *Ghostbusters* (1984)

Quincy Jones, Lionel Ritchie, and Rod Temperton, "Miss Celie's Blues" from *The Color Purple* (1985)

Jonas Gwangwa, "Cry Freedom" from *Cry Freedom* (1987)

Jimmy Jam, Terry Lewis and Janet Jackson, "Again" from *Poetic Justice* (1993)

James Ingram, "The Day I Fall in Love" from *Beethoven's 2nd* (1993)

James Ingram, "Look What Love Has Done" from *Junior* (1995)

Siedah Garrett, "Love You I Do" from *Dreamgirls* (2006)

Jamal Joseph, Charles Mack and Tevin Thomas, "Raise It Up" from *August Rush* (2007)

Siedah Garrett, "Real in Rio" from *Rio* (2011)

Pharrell Williams, "Happy" from *Despicable Me 2* (2013)

Academy Award Winner for Best Documentary Feature

T.J. Martin, *Undefeated* (2012)

Academy Award Nominee for Best Documentary Feature

Yvonne Smith (producer), Adam Clayton Powell (1990)

Spike Lee (director) and Samuel D. Pollard (producer), *4 Little Girls* (1997)

Karolyn Ali (producer), *Tupac: Resurrection* (2004)

Black Filmmakers Hall of Fame

1973
Clarence Muse (1889-1910)
Gordon Parks (1912-2006)

1974
Katherine Dunham (1909-2006)
Lincoln "Stepin Fetchit" Perry (1902-1985)
Paul Robeson (1898-1976)

1975
Ruby Dee (1922-2014)
Allen Hoskins (1920-1980)
Hall Johnson (1888-1970)
Abbey Lincoln (1930-2010)
Hattie McDaniel (1895-1952)
Butterfly McQueen (1911-1995)
Fredi Washington (1903 - 1994)

1976
Eubie Blake (1887-1983)
Louise Beavers (1902-1962)
Oscar Micheaux (1884-1951)
Brock Peters (1927-2005)
Melvin Van Peebles (b. 1932)
Diahann Carroll (b. 1935)

1977
Maidie Norman (1912-1998)
Cicely Tyson (b. 1933)

1978
Benny Carter (1907-2003)
Nina Mae McKinney (1912-1967)
Sidney Poitier (b. 1927)
Fayard (1914-2006) & Harold (1921-2000)
Nicholas

1979
Etta Moten Barnett (1901-2004)
Kath "Oodgeroo Noonuccal" Walker
  (1920-1993)

1980
Ivan Dixon (1931-2008)
William Greaves (1926-2014)

1984
Billy Dee Williams (b. 1937)

1986
Nellie "Madame Sul-Te-Wan" Crawford
  (1873-1959)

1987
Sammy Davis, Jr. (1925-1990)
Scatman Crothers (1910-1986)
Jeni Le Gon (1916 -2012)
Ernie Morrison (1912-1989)

1990
Suzanne de Passe (b. 1948)
Danny Glover (b. 1946)

1991
Michael Schultz (b. 1938)
August Wilson (1945-2005)

1993
Madeline Anderson
Rosalind Cash (1938-1995)

1995
William D. Alexander (1916-1991)

Made in the USA
Coppell, TX
31 October 2021